Srimad Bhagvadgita

Srimad Bhagavadgita
A Treatise on Counselling
A Psychological Study

K. Ramakrishna Rao

GITAM
(Deemed to be University)

PRINTWORLD
Publishers of Indian Traditions

Cataloging in Publication Data — DK
[Courtesy: D.K. Agencies (P) Ltd. <docinfo@dkagencies.com>]

Rao, K. Ramakrishna, author.
Srimad Bhagavadgita : a treatise on counselling : a psychological study / K. Ramakrishna Rao.
pages cm
Includes index.
ISBN 9788124609682

1. Bhagavadgītā – Psychology. 2. Hinduism – Psychology. 3. Counseling psychology. 4. Yoga. 5. Self-actualization (Psychology) in literature. I. GITAM University. II. Title.

LCC BL1138.66.R36 2019 | DDC 294.5924046 23

ISBN: 978-81-246-0968-2
First published in India in 2019

Printed and published by:
D.K. Printworld (P) Ltd.
Regd. Office: "Vedaśrī", F-395, Sudarshan Park
(Metro Station: E.S.I. Hospital), New Delhi - 110015
Phones: (011) 2545 3975, 2546 6019
e-mail: indology@dkprintworld.com
Website: www.dkprintworld.com

To

My loving wife,

Sarojini

a fountain of joy and devoted companion

for seven decades and continuing

Preface

My academic clock has run the full cycle. Began with an interest in Indian thought and a desire for finding my intellectual and cultural roots, I became completely Westernized without realizing it at the time. It was my involvement in parapsychology and the hope of finding a scientific bridge between the Eastern and Western thought that transformed a tender-minded, philosophically oriented person into a tough experimental scientist under the influence of J.B. Rhine. Now, more than one half a century after I began my journey which covered mostly the Western ground, I return with a bang with a vigorous revival of interest in and unwavering commitment to my native tradition. This book is one of the outcomes.

The other major development is my involvement in the revival of Indian psychology, psychology rooted in classical Indian thought. This is in some ways a pioneering endeavour along with a few other like-minded psychologists. If successful, it would bring a paradigm shift in the fundamental postulates of psychological theory and empirical studies derived from them.

At long last, I am now finding my Indian roots. Doing this book is not merely a matter of good intellectual exercise, but also a very satisfying emotional experience. I read the *Gita* several times earlier. However, the present exercise is more than *understanding*; it is acquisition of wisdom and involves some kind of *realization*, which in my view is the ultimate destiny of all learning.

There are many English translations of the *Gita*. It is my hope that this book offers a little more than merely translating each verse into readable English. With emphasis on the meaning and not on the structure of each verse, we endeavour to reach out to English knowing readers, especially those with interest in psychology.

This book is my modest attempt to provide a psychological rendering of the *Gita* with focus on its implications to counselling. In this exercise I have benefitted much by some of the earlier commentators on the *Gita* in English such as Balgangadhar Tilak, Mahatma Gandhi and Sarvepalli Radhakrishnan. Of course, I was also inspired by some of the classical commentators such as Shankaracharya.

There are several colleagues and associates who helped me in various ways in completing this work. A special mention may be made of Dr Rositta Joseph who copy-edited the manuscript with meticulous care, generously giving a lot of her time. My secretary Mrs Prasanna Kumari spared no effort to do her best. However, if there are any shortcomings, I take the full responsibility for them.

As always, my trusted publisher and friend Shri

Susheel K. Mittal of the D.K. Printworld has done an outstanding job in giving this book an attractive look in print. I hope he will be amply rewarded for his enthusiastic endeavour to promote Indian studies.

K. Ramakrishna Rao
Chancellor
GITAM (deemed to be) University

Contents

Introduction

This book is a modest attempt to bring out some of the psychological insights in the *Gita* into focus. It addresses primarily those psychologists who are unfamiliar with the rich psychological heritage in the classical Indian tradition.

In rendering the *Gita* verses into English, I was guided more by the meaning of the message contained, rather than concerned with providing a literal translation. I paid little attention to the syntax and the structure of the sentence, concentrating almost wholly on the semantic spirit of each verse. Further, I made a concerted effort to make the verses easily readable by and understandable to non-scholars in the Indic tradition, and especially to students of psychology. Therefore, my psychological rendering of the verses of the *Gita* may not be syntactically intact vis-à-vis the original; but I did everything I could to be semantically faithful to the text. I have learned much from other commentators and translators of the *Gita* in English such as Tilak, Gandhi and Radhakrishnan.

S. Radhakrishnan in the "Introductory Essay"[1]

---

[1] Radhakrishnan, S., 1948/1963, *Bhagavadgita: With an Introductory Essay, Sanskrit Text, English Translation and Notes*, pp. 11-78, London: George Allen & Unwin.

accompanying his translation of the *Bhagavadgita* observed that the *Gita* is more a religious classic than a philosophical treatise. However, he went on to expound the ethical and metaphysical significance of the *Gita.* Following Sir Sarvepalli's lead, we endeavour to bring out in this volume the lessons that psychologists may learn from the *Gita.* I consider the *Bhagavadgita* a sourcebook of counselling psychology in the Indian tradition. It is equally a relevant text for *understanding* human nature in general.

The context of the *Gita* from a psychological perspective is mental conflict, a clash of possible courses of action. From an ethical viewpoint, it is a fight between good and evil. The scene is the battle between the virtuous and the wicked. The stage is the chariot, Lord Krishna, the divine in human form, is driving with Arjuna, the warrior behind, who represents the human instincts that drive the mind. Figuratively, Arjuna represents the human mind and its instinctive animal drives and Krishna stands for divine aspirations behind one's endeavour. Man is a composite of the animal and the divine. This is an observation that Mahatma Gandhi has repeatedly made. It may also be considered as a fundamental postulate of Indian psychology.

The *Gita,* which stands out as the centrepiece of the Indian epic the *Mahabharata,* is a dialogue between Arjuna, an accomplished warrior, presently troubled by a confused and paralysed mind, and Lord Krishna helping to clear Arjuna's mind and set him on the right course, as narrated by Sanjaya to Dhritarashtra, the blind king and patriarch of the Kauravas. Sanjaya represents that aspect of the mind capable of reflection and introspection enabling one to transcend the ego and subjectivity and get closer to the truth. In a figurative sense, the blind Dhritarashtra was unable to discriminate between what is right and what is wrong. He was ego-driven and anxious to know what was happening on the battlefield and whether his sons would be victorious. Sanjaya stands for the opposite, a virtuous and truthful person who has overcome human weaknesses such as attachment and repulsion; and therefore is able to make an objective presentation of what actually is the case. It is an illustration of a man who is blind to the virtues and the one who has discriminating wisdom to distinguish the right and the worthy from the false and the immoral.

The first chapter of the *Gita* depicts the despondency of Arjuna, paralysed by conflicting thoughts as mentioned. The human mind has in its very nature the propensity to wander. Therefore, it needs to be anchored to a firm faith in and commitment to certain values. Arjuna saw those in front of him, whom he was expected to attack and kill. However, the Kauravas facing him in the battlefield happened to be his own kith and kin with whom Arjuna had family bonds. Here was a manifest conflict of values. On the one hand, it was Arjuna's duty as a kshatriya to fight in the battlefield and kill if necessary; and on the other hand, loving one's kin is the characteristic of any noble person. We do not kill our own people even if they are on the wrong side. It was this conflict and agony that the dispirited Arjuna shared with Sri Krishna on the battlefield of Kurukshetra.

The *Bhagavadgita* is Krishna's counsel to help Arjuna overcome the conflict and play his role as a warrior engaged in a noble battle, ignoring for the moment his kinship with Kauravas. Therefore, at the heart of the *Bhagavadgita*, we have the theme of psychological counselling to give stability and direction to a confused mind. It is indeed much like a therapeutic situation, where the therapist tries to bring clarity to an unclear mind and guide the person towards the correct and appropriate course of action in actual life. Arjuna is the client and Krishna takes the role of a therapeutic counsellor. The *Gita* is more than simple counselling. We may see in it an exercise in life-transforming cognitive psychotherapy. It is indeed a perennial discourse that shows the path towards self-actualization.

1

The Existential Anguish

The Depression and Despondency of Arjuna

In the Indian tradition, man is seen as situated in a sea of suffering. This is the *existential anguish*. Man's endeavour is to swim to the shores of bliss. This is the *existential quest*. The *Bhagavadgita* is a poetic depiction of the anguish and the quest set in the context of a battlefield. The battlefield is not only the physical war ground but also the mental arena filled with conflicting thoughts.

The first verse of the *Gita* begins with the blind King Dhritarashtra asking Sanjaya, his interpreter:

VERSE 1

> In the field of righteousness (*dharmakshetra*) and the land of Kurus (Kurukshetra) what did my sons and the children of Pandu do, facing each other in the battlefield, tell me Oh Sanjaya.

VERSES 2-9

Sanjaya replies

> Having looked at the formation of the army of Pandavas, Prince Duryodhana approached his teacher Dronacharya and said:

> Behold, Oh preceptor, look at the vast army of Pandu's children guided by your gifted disciple, the son of Drupada. Here are courageous, mighty warriors, such as Bhima and Arjuna, Yuyudhana, Virata and Drupada, Dhrishtaketu, Cekitana and the King of Kaṣhi as well as Purujit, Kuntibhoja and Shaibya. Further, there are other outstanding warriors Yudhamanyu, Uttamauja, Abhimanyu (the son of Arjuna and Subhadra), and sons of Draupadi.

These persons stand for one set of factors acting on the human mind in a conflict situation.

> On our side, we have besides you, Bhishma, Karna, Kripa, Ashvatthama, Vikarna, and also the son of Somadatta and many other warriors.

These individuals refer to the opposing set of factors in a conflict. We may note in this context that these are not necessarily bad and wicked people as opposed to the other. Some of them are indeed very virtuous, but they were either misguided or chose to be on the wrong side for other compelling reasons of their own. So a conflict situation is not an either/or event where all people on one side are necessarily good and those on the other side are bad and wicked. Rather, people on both sides are driven and guided at a given moment by one set of factors neglecting others. Similar is the case with the human mind. It attends to some events ignoring or actively suppressing some others, driven at a given moment by a variety of factors acting on it. The suppressed ones are not intrinsically bad and the expressed ones necessarily good.

VERSE 10

> Our army led by Bhishma is vast, but not adequate; and the forces led by Bhima are limited but sufficient.

It is suggested here that the human mind is overwhelmed by various conflicting thoughts. However, those leading one on the right course may be a few and limited, whereas the misleading ones many and widespread. It conveys that the unlimited army of Bhishma on hand may be inadequate whereas the limited forces available to Bhima are quite sufficient to battle successfully. The lesson is that mere numbers by themselves do not count. What is implied here is that what matters in the final analysis is the conviction and not sheer numbers. The psychological import of this verse is that a properly functioning mind requires not a multitude of wavering ideas but a well motivated resolve to execute the chosen one.

VERSE 11

> Stationed at all points of entry and exit, maintaining due order you all provide protection to Bhishma.

The emphasis here is on the outward forces acting on and guarding the mind; and not the inner drive of the person. This was Duryodhana's posture with an emphasis on the physical and the outer world. It is a psychologically weak approach, a prelude to the impending disaster and defeat.

VERSES 12-13

> To the delight of Duryodhana, the grand old mighty Bhishma, roaring like a lion, blew his conch.

> Then there was a tumultuous din with the sounding of conches, drums, cymbals and trumpets.

Bhishma was driven more by his duty of leading the Kaurava army and not by an inner conviction that he was on the right path. All the noise refers to the unruly thoughts and indiscriminate action that followed.

VERSES 14-19

> Riding a large chariot drawn by white horses Krishna and Arjuna blew their divine conchs, Krishna his Panchajanya and Arjuna his Devadatta. Bhima known for his mighty deeds and enormous appetite blew his Paundra. Yudhishthira, the eldest of Pandavas, sounded his Ananta-Vijaya followed by his youngest brothers Nakula and Sahadeva, the king of Kashi, Shikhandi, Dhrishtadyumna, Virata, Satyaki, Drupada, the sons of Draupadi, and the son of Subhadra who blew their conches from all sides. Tumultuous uproar reverberated through the earth and the sky ripping the hearts of the Kauravas.

These verses describe the people on the side of the Pandavas who represent the virtuous and noble manifesting desirable virtues and values. White stands for purity and virtuosity. These verses also emphasize the need for and ways to control the wandering mind.

VERSES 20-25

> Arjuna with Hanuman on his flag had a glance at the army opposing him and the criss-cross of fire between them. He asked Krishna to move his chariot between

> the two armies to enable him to have a good look at those on the side of the evil-minded Duryodhana, son of Dhritarashtra. Then, Krishna moved the chariot to a position between the two armies. He told Arjuna, "See those Kauravas gathered here to wage a war against you."

This passage depicts the introspective aspect of the human mind eager to learn about what is actually happening at a given moment of time. Such a prelude is an essential aspect of taking the necessary and effective course of action. It specifically calls attention to the factors and forces that one needs to familiarize himself with before he begins his pursuit.

VERSES 26-30

> Arjuna saw his grandfathers, brothers, teachers, cousins, nephews, grandsons, fathers-in-law, and friends involved in the two armies facing each other to fight. Overwhelmed by immense grief and sorrow and supreme compassion, Arjuna said to Krishna "My limbs falter, my mouth has become dry, my body shivers, and the hairs stand on end. The bow slips from my hand, my skin is burning, my hands tremble, and I am unable to stand upright."

This passage, depicting Arjuna's predicament and his perplexed mind, is full of psychological significance. It describes what happens to one when he is overwhelmed by emotion in a conflict situation. It narrates the psycho-physiological states associated with severe stress.

VERSES 31-46

> Oh Krishna, I see unwholesome signs; and see no good in killing my own people. I do not crave for victory, power or pleasures. The people we care for are standing in front of us willing to sacrifice their lives and wealth. They include teachers, fathers and even grandfathers, grandchildren, and other kith and kin. I do not wish to kill them, even if they stand there to kill me. What do we gain by killing them except sin? What good will come out of this bloodshed? What do we expect to achieve by marching on the bodies of the dead who are dear to us? It does not seem right to kill our own people. No matter if those on the other side are driven by greed and do not really care about their friends and family. May we not be wise to avoid that kind of sin?
>
> Destruction of one's family entails violation of laws bequeathed by tradition. When laws are violated, lawlessness ensues. Our tradition exemplifies the mature will and wholesome experience of generations of people. Laws are meant to protect the tradition; and when the lawlessness prevails, the society gets corrupted. The family is the pivot; a stable society moves on it. When the family's tradition is uprooted and the social equilibrium is disturbed, there will be chaos in the world. It will be hell. It would be a great sin if we strive to slay our own people prompted by the greed to enjoy the pleasures of victory. I would feel better if I, with no arms in hand and unresisting, am attacked and killed on the battlefield.

This passage is an eloquent statement of Arjuna's

predicament and existential anguish. It suggests that a paradigmatic shift in one's outlook may be called for to pursue a suggested course of action, which is counter to his tradition. It is a persuasive defence of tradition. It shows the enormity of the task ahead of the counsellor to change the mindset of his client and help resolve a genuine conflict. The manifest conflict in the mind of Arjuna is not that of a sick man, which would have been easier to deal with. Rather it indicates a genuine and natural conflict between tradition and the impending changes. What Arjuna needs is a new orientation that helps to find a synthesis of the dialectic of conflicting thoughts, reasonable and desirable on the one hand and harmful and not so ethical on the other.

VERSE 47

> Having said this, Arjuna, dispirited and overwhelmed by sorrow fell back in his seat, dropping his bow and arrow.

The first chapter of the *Gita* thus depicts the depression and despondency of Arjuna. There are many lessons here for psychologists to learn. First and foremost is the well-rounded phenomenology of depression experienced by a normal and mentally sound individual under the stress of conflict between tradition and the contemplated course of action. This poses formidable problems and challenges for the counsellor under such circumstances. What is needed is imparting overwhelming wisdom to overcome the opposing thoughts by finding a viable synthesis. This is the formidable task of the divine counsellor, Krishna.

2

Yoga Theory : Practice and Outcome

Continuing his narrative, Sanjaya added:

VERSES 1-9

Krishna said to the depressed and sorrowful Arjuna who had his eyes filled with tears and was overcome with self pity:

> Why are you so dejected at this time of crisis? Such dejection is alien to nobility. It does not lead one to heaven; it brings disgrace. Such pitiful posture is unmanly and not befitting you. Rise up, Oh Partha, the nightmare of the foes.

Unpersuaded, Arjuna continued:

> Krishna, Oh the slayer of foes, how can I aim my arrows to kill Bhishma and Drona who are worthy of worship?
>
> I would feel better to make a living by begging than killing these revered teachers. By slaying them I would enjoy a life smeared with blood.
>
> Under these circumstances, I am unable to know whether it is better to conquer them or let them conquer us. Those we are facing on the battlefield are those by killing whom we do not wish to live.
>
> My mind striken by self pity, confused, bewildered is unable to grasp where my duty lies, I beg you to tell

me, what to do. I am your pupil, pray, teach me. I am seeking refuge in you.

I am unable to understand how I may overcome this sorrow drenching my senses by becoming rich, enjoying unrivalled kingdom on earth, or even by conquering the gods. How would I live happily? I cannot fight this battle. Saying this Arjuna became silent.

These nine verses refer to fundamental epistemological issues, and raise basic questions relating to one's thought and action. They reflect the manifest conflict between diverse forces acting on the mind. They are the prelude to the exposition to follow on the theory and practice of *yoga* to control the wanderings of the mind.

Speaking to the blind king Dhritarashtra, Sanjaya continued his narration of what was happening on the battlefield.

VERSE 10

To the depressed Arjuna standing between the two armies poised to fight, Krishna said with a mocking smile[1] on his face.

VERSES 11-39

You speak of wisdom; and then go on to grieve for those you should not grieve for. People with wisdom do not grieve either for the dead or the living.

There was no time when we did not exist; there would

[1] Mocking smile is the prelude to what Krishna is going to say.

be no time when we cease to exist.

Wise men know that just as it travels with the body in all its stages from childhood to old age, the soul moves on to take another body, when the previous body ceases to exist. While the soul is eternal, none of its embodiments is permanent.

Contacts with the objects of the world give rise to physical sensations such as hot and cold, and mental states like pain and pleasure. These come and go, and do not last forever. We should learn to endure them when they come, Oh Arjuna.

The person, who is untroubled by these passing events and wise to remain unaffected by them, overcomes suffering forever and finds his eternal place.

Those that exit will never cease to be; and those that do not exist never come to be. This fact is attested by those who see the truth.

All that pervades the universe is immutable and therefore indestructible. The changeless never perishes.

It is believed that the perishable bodies belong to the embodied self. The *self* itself is eternal, imperishable and indeed indeterminable. So, Arjuna, go on and fight.

There is no one who kills or is killed. The one who thinks otherwise fails to comprehend the truth.

The real within is never born; and has no death. *Self* is eternal, primordial and permanent.

How can one destroy the imperishable, undecaying,

unborn and eternal? Who is there to kill or to be killed?

The *self* leaves the tired and unfit bodies, like the person casts off worn out clothes.

Arrows do not pierce the *self*; fire cannot burn it. Rains do not get it wet. Nor do winds dry it up.

Being eternal, all-pervading, unchanging and immovable, the *self* is beyond the ravages of weather and immune from destruction.

Knowing that the *self* is unmanifest and immutable, one does not grieve because it is not perishable.

Even if you believe that the *self* is repeatedly born and perpetually undergoes death, you should not grieve.

One who is born is certain to die; and it is equally true that death is followed by birth. Consequently you should not grieve for what is inevitable.

Beings have no form either in the beginning or in the end. The form is manifest only in the middle. Therefore, what is there to lament?

People look at the *self* as a marvel, but they seldom know what it is.

The *self*, which dwells in every one's body, is eternal and cannot be killed. Consequently, there is nothing to grieve for anyone.

Moreover, keeping in mind your duty as a kshatriya, you should not waver to fight in the battlefield. A kshatriya should feel happy because a war such as this opens up for him the doors to heaven.

> If you do not fight this lawful war, you would be failing in your duty, lose the glory, and incur sin.
>
> Further, you become infamous. For an honourable person such ill-fame is worse than death.
>
> To the legendary warriors, you would appear as a coward, who abstained from battle out of fear; and those who had high esteem for you now would not take you seriously any more.
>
> Your enemies mocking at you would say many slanderous words you do not deserve. What could be more sad than this?
>
> If you are killed in the battlefield, you would go to heaven. If you become victorious, you would enjoy the pleasures of the earth. Therefore, Oh Arjuna, go on and fight.
>
> If you treat pain and pleasure, loss and gain, defeat and victory alike, you would not incur any sin.
>
> This is what the wise men of Samkhya have to say. Now, let me describe to you what *yoga* is.

So far, Krishna's counsel was aimed at convincing Arjuna by appeal to his intellect. Now he moves on to counsel from other angles. The shift is from head to the heart, from theory to practice. Samkhya is the intellectual ground and Yoga involves cultivation of true wisdom. The two go together in the Indian tradition; and the *Bhagavadgita* is an epitome of Indian wisdom. The verses are the capsules containing a marvellous mix of thought and action and a splendid blend of morality and metaphysics.

VERSES 40-54

The path of *yoga* is the way of action. Travelling on this path does no harm.

Even a little practice of this *dharma* saves one from peril and frees him from fear and failure.

The *yoga* of action involves focused and unwavering attention. The unfocused mind harbours numerous undiscerning thoughts.

The unwise revel in the flowery letters of the Veda and think that there is nothing else beyond it to know.

Such people are reborn to reap the fruits of their actions.

Despite their ability to grasp the difference between what is right and what is wrong, those carried away by sensuous pleasures and driven by desire for power cannot have focused mind necessary for self-actualization.

Vedas point to a threefold way for self-actualization. It involves (a) overcoming the dualities one confronts, (b) being ethical and free from desire to acquire and accumulate, and finally (c) gaining insight into the *self*.

As is the case with the pond that stores the inundating flood water, so do the Vedas harness the flow of wisdom and truth.

We have the freedom to act, but not the rights to its fruits. There should be no attachment either to action or inaction.

Yoga stabilizes the mind and makes it steadfast.

> Engaged in *yoga*, one should eschew attachment and treat success and failure alike with an even mind.
>
> Action guided by its expected fruits is far inferior to the understanding of the equipoised and unattached mind. Cultivate such a balanced and stable mind, Arjuna, and pity those who hanker after the fruits of their actions.
>
> With steady mind be indifferent to the good and bad deeds of others and strive to do your duty. This is *yoga*; *yoga* gives added skill in one's work.
>
> Men with equanimous mind who are detached and pay no attention to the fruits of their actions are liberated from the bondage of birth and become free from all suffering.
>
> When your mind thus transcends all attachments and pays no need to what is heard and may be heard, and stands firm, unshaken, and stable, you enter the state of yogic *samadhi.*
>
> In the state of *samadhi*, the mind becomes stable and focused, leading to self-actualization, which is the final destination of men of wisdom.
>
> Arjuna then asked Krishna to describe for him the physical posture and the mental characteristics of such a self-actualized person (*sthitaprajna*):
>
> How does he speak, sit and walk?

The above verses show that Krishna has succeeded in opening up the mind of Arjuna, who is now ready to listen to the former's counsel. This is an important stage in the counselling process. The client comes with a lot of baggage of preconceived notions, beliefs and expectations. They need to be first cleared before proceeding further. What follows is the central message of the *Gita* that succinctly describes the quintessential characteristics of a self-actualized person. From a therapeutic perspective, it shows the significance of the firm theoretical foundation to build one's belief structure and a stable mind to arrive at a workable synthesis of conflicting thoughts.

Human beings are a composite of the beast and the Divine. The human pursuit is to overcome the beastly nature and to seek the Divine within. Self-actualization involves the realization of the Divine within. The characteristics described below are the attributes of a self-actualized person.

VERSES 56-72

> The self-actualized person is stable and steadfast. His mind is equanimous, undisturbed by sorrows; it is unmoved by desire for sensuous pleasures, and is free from fear, attachment and repulsion.
>
> His mind is set firmly in wisdom. He does not rejoice when good things happen or get dejected when evil acts manifest.
>
> He withdraws his senses and abstains from their pleasures, just like a tortoise rests his limbs in the shell.
>
> One may abstain from sensory indulgence; and yet the taste of its pleasures may continue to linger in the mind. A self-actualized person becomes free

even from traces of such tastes and their lingering memories.

Even though one may relentlessly strive for and be ever so perceptive, the mind may be carried away by the emotional forces unleashed by the senses.

Therefore, one needs to firmly set his anchor in *yoga* with full faith in the Divine.

When the mind indulges in sensory acts, attachment for them arises. Attachment engenders desires. From desires come frustrations; and frustrations lead to anger.

Anger gives rise to confusion and bewilderment. Such bewilderment and perplexity cause lose of memory. From memory loss, intelligence is disturbed and wisdom is lost; and with it one perishes.

However, a person with a steadfast, focused and stable *mind,* who is engaged with the objects of sense without attachment or aversion, achieves purity of mind.

With that purity, comes the end of all sorrow; and the person is led on the path of self-actualization.

With no control of the senses, there would be no control of the mind. Without the needed control over the senses, one fails to control the functions of the mind and is unable to concentrate. Without concentration, there is no peace of mind. Without peace of mind, there could be no happiness.

The mind driven by wandering senses seeking physical pleasures fails to have right perceptions just as the ship tossed by winds goes off its course.

> Therefore, Oh Arjuna, a self-actualized person withdraws fully his senses from the objects.
>
> Things would look different to one who achieves self-actualization. What is night to ordinary people, would be full of light to one who is awakened. What is the day for ordinary folks, the enlightened persons see its dark side.
>
> Unlike the one who is engulfed in desires, the person whose streams of desire flow into the tranquil sea of consciousness, achieves peace.
>
> The one, who transcends his ego, is free from all longings, and gives up all desires, attains peace.
>
> In the divine state of self-actualization, there is no bewilderment. Fixed in that state, when one leaves the body, he attains full divinity.

These verses succinctly summarize the characteristics of a self-actualized person. Briefly, the message is that the self-actualized person realizes his true *self* as distinct from the ego, transcends all sensory cravings and becomes detached from the fruits of action. Such a person is unbound and finds his way to liberation and thus participates in divinity, which is to rise above the animal instincts and undergo spiritual transformation. His life epitomizes happiness in its best sense.

3

Yoga of Action

ARJUNA was not yet fully convinced. Doubts still lingered in his mind. So, he went on to ask Krishna:

> If you consider that knowing is better than doing, why then are you, Krishna, persuading me to indulge in this savage action?
>
> Further, you confuse me by making apparently conflicting statements. Pray, tell me unequivocally what is it I should do in order to achieve the highest good?

Krishna responds:

> Oh, Arjuna, I mentioned to you earlier the twofold way of life – one of knowledge and the other of action. The path of knowledge is best suited for those with a disposition to contemplate; and the way of work is best for the people with a tendency for action.
>
> A man does not become fully free either by engaging in action or by simply renouncing it.
>
> No person can remain even for a moment without doing something because it is in his very nature; it is his natural impulse to act. He is impelled to act because he is a manifestation of the three *gunas* - *sattva, rajas,* and *tamas.*
>
> He who abstains from action, but continues to long

for sensory enjoyment is a deluded person. In short, he is a hypocrite.

However, the one who overcomes sensory indulgence and yet gets involved in action without attachment is a *karma-yogi*. He is a far superior being.

Engaging in action is better than doing nothing; we cannot sustain even our physical form without work.

There is no bondage for the person who performs his duties without attachment or repulsion. His work does not stand in the way to his liberation. Therefore, Arjuna, do your work with the spirit of sacrifice without any form of attachment.

In the beginning, God created the humankind stating "with this form you may satisfy your desires".

In this form you may worship gods and they may take care of you. By such mutual fostering, you shall reach the supreme heights.

Pleased by their offerings, gods will grant people the pleasures they seek. The person who enjoys these pleasures just for himself without giving to others is no better than a thief.

The people, who eat what is left after feeding others, are not sinful. However, those, who have the food just for themselves, literally eat sin. They are wicked and utterly devoid of any merit.

Food generates and sustains life. Rain helps to produce food. Rains come from the services we render. Our service to others involves work.

All action has its roots in the *Brahman*; and the

Brahman is imperishable and all-pervading. He is firmly founded in services devoid of attachment.

He who does not turn with this wheel of *dharma* and instead engages in sensuous enjoyment is evil in nature, incurs sin, and lives a wasted life.

However, for the self-actualized person who is fully content and satisfied, there is no further work to be done to attain freedom.

Further, with no interest in the worldly things and not expecting any benefit from the present or future actions, he has no motivation or need for action. Action for him is *sui generis*.

Do your work always without attachment. Man reaches his highest state of self-actualization by doing his work without attachment.

It was through relentless work and not seeking reward that people like King Janaka became self-actualized persons.

Whatever famous men do, the others try to follow. Great men set standards for others to emulate.

Oh Arjuna, there is no work to be done by me in this or the other worlds. There is nothing I have not achieved or want to achieve. Yet, I am engaged in work.

It is so because if I ever fail to engage in work untired, other men follow me.

If I should cease to work, this world would be in ruins. I would be creating chaos and cause destruction.

Unlike the ignorant who act with attachment, the

learned persons work without attachment and with intention to maintain order and sustain the world.

Let the man of understanding and insight arouse the minds of the ignorant. An enlightened person should set the example for others to work in the spirit of service.

The ego-driven person thinks that he is the doer when in fact all manifest work is an expression inherent in nature.

On the other hand, those who understand the underlying distinction between the spirit and the material body do not become attached.

Those who are deluded by the appearance of things get attached. However, those who know the entire truth may not attempt to instantly fix the minds of those with only partial understanding.

By surrendering to the divine with a spiritual frame of mind that does not crave, is free from the ego and gives up all possessions, Oh Arjuna, fight unconcerned.

Those with full faith in me and free from petty concerns follow the divine injunctions and are liberated from their earthly bondages.

However, those who do their duties without regard to the Divine are ignorant, blind to truth, and senseless.

Even knowledgeable men and indeed all beings follow their nature. What can repression of natural tendencies accomplish?

All the senses by their very nature are attracted or repulsed by the objects they encounter. Things that stand in the way are the way layers.

It is better to do one's own duty, even if it is done imperfectly than discharging another's task with perfection. It is perilous to prefer another's duty to one's own.

Arjuna then asks Krishna:

What is it that impels a man to commit sin even against his own wish?

Krishna answers:

It is the craving, over powering anger born of the *rajas guna* in his nature. Such craving is sinful. Realize that it is your enemy.

Craving clouds knowledge, like the womb hides the embryo and dirt obscures the images in the mirror.

Insatiable desires are the haunting enemies of those seeking wisdom.

The senses, the mind, and the accompanying intelligence are the seats of desires. They hide wisdom and lead to worldly delusions.

Therefore, Arjuna, bring your senses under control and put to rest those standing in the way of discriminating wisdom.

It is said that the senses are great. Greater than the senses is the mind. Even more important than the mind is intelligence. However, the spirit is more noble than them all.

It follows, then, that restraining the senses, overcoming the mental distractions and focusing on the true spirit inside is the way to get rid of craving, the enemy within.

Krishna thus instructed Arjuna to act and perform his duties as a warrior in the midst of war. These are words full of psychological wisdom. They suggest how the therapist may persuade his reluctant client to change his mindset and do the right thing instead of withdrawing from action and become depressed. The essence of this chapter is the assertion of the importance and virtues of detached action.

4

Jnana-Yoga

Krishna went on to enlighten Arjuna about the way of knowledge to achieve self-actualization. He said:

> I taught to the Sun the way of knowledge for self-realization, who imparted it to Manu. Manu in turn passed it on to Ikshvaku.
>
> This has been traditionally transmitted by royal sages to their descendants. However, over a period of long time, this *yoga* lost its ground.
>
> Now I am teaching it to you because you are my friend and devotee. Knowledge of this *yoga* remained a great mystery for a long time.

Arjuna asked Krishna:

> You are clearly born much later than the Sun. How, then is it that you are the first to teach this *yoga*?

Krishna responded thus:

> I was born many times before. So were you. I am aware of them all; but you are not.
>
> Though I am the unborn and unchanging Self, it is by my power of becoming (*maya*) I take different forms.
>
> Whenever, morality is threatened and *adharma* is on the rise, Arjuna, I come into being in the world.
>
> In order to protect the righteous persons and punish the wicked people, I am born in every age.

Those who truly become aware of my divinity become self-actualized persons. They no longer go through the cycle of birth and death.

Freed from passion, fear, and anger by true wisdom and getting absorbed in divinity, they become self-actualized persons.

Whatever the manner people may seek divinity, they achieve it; and people have many ways of approaching the Divine.

Desiring success in their action, people make offerings to gods. In the existential context, success comes quick in such pursuits; but it does not last for long.

There is a divine sanction for the fourfold social order. Though I created that order, I am incapable of changing it.

Actions do not taint those who have no longing for their fruits. People who know and practise this are unbound by their actions.

Our ancestors seeking liberation thus worked without going after its fruits. You also should follow this hoary tradition of ours.

What is really the distinction between action and inaction? This is a question that bewildered even the wise sages. I shall presently explain to you what one needs to know in order to overcome evil.

It is paramount that people know the difference between work and bad action. Further, they need to be aware of what inaction it involves. The course of work is indeed profound.

The person who sees action in inaction and inaction in action, he is wise and an accomplished *yogin.*

Those who act with discriminating insight and whose desires are consumed in the fire of knowledge are truly the men of wisdom.

The man, who is detached from the fruits of action, content, and self-reliant without depending on others, is unbound.

With no desires to seek, self-satisfied, and being non-possessive, the person who engages in action does no wrong and therefore he is not bound.

The one, who is satisfied with what comes his way, becomes indifferent to all dualities like pain and pleasure, has no jealousy, and looks at success and failure with equanimity, is not bound by his actions.

Detached from desires, focused on truth, the one who does his work as service is not bound by his actions. He becomes a self-actualized person.

Such a person focuses on the divine, seeks the divine, and sees the divine in his work and thus realizes divinity.

Some *yogins* render service to please gods, while others get absorbed by the knowledge of the Divine.

Some sacrifice their senses in order to achieve mental restraint. Some others prevent the objects from reaching the senses.

Yet others give up all sensory indulgence by gaining appropriate knowledge.

Further, there are those who expend their material possessions in the spirit of service. They observe austerities or engage in spiritual exercises to actualize themselves.

Some practise control of breathing, restrain both breathing in and breathing out. They achieve a state of breath suspension called *kumbhaka.*

Yet others, engage themselves in diet control and fasting. By such sacrifices, they attempt to eradicate their sins.

Those, who are content with eating whatever remains after others eat, become self-actualized persons. This world is not fit for those who do not partake in such sacrifices. How can they hope to reach other worlds?

A variety of sacrifices are described in the Vedas. All of them involve action. By realizing this truth one becomes free.

Offering of knowledge is superior to material offerings, sacrifice, because all action without exception has wisdom as its goal.

Men of wisdom tell us that one could become free by service, devotion or knowledge.

When you know this truth, Arjuna, you will no longer be confused. You will realize how all that exists is contained in the divinity of the *self.*

Even if you are situated in the sea of sins, you will overcome all evil and reach the shores of your liberation by the boat of wisdom.

Like the fire which reduces the things that it touches

> into ashes, so does knowledge turn all action into ashes.
>
> There is nothing that liberates one better than knowledge. By practising *yoga* one realizes this in course of time.
>
> Through devotion one is able to control his senses and get absorbed in knowledge. By gaining and mastering knowledge one achieves the state of self-actualization.
>
> However, the person devoid of wisdom, who has no faith and engages in doubts is lost.
>
> The one who renounces action following *yoga*, and who overcomes doubt with wisdom realizes his true self.
>
> Give up the doubts that arise due to ignorance, take on the task on hand and follow the path of wisdom. Get ready, Arjuna, and fight.

The above passages depict modes of persuasion to convince the client to overcome the conflicts, get out of depression and act with a positive mindset. The main thesis is that knowledge is the true way to gain self-realization, even though action and devotion have their due role in achieving the state of self-actualization.

5

Yoga of Renunciation

VERSES 1-19

STILL not fully convinced Arjuna asked Krishna:

> Oh Krishna you preach me on the one hand to relinquish all action and extol on the other hand to act unselfishly. Please clarify which of the two is better.

Krishna said:

> Renunciation of action as well as selfless action lead the person towards liberation. However, unselfish actions are better than their renunciation.
>
> He, who neither shuns nor is swayed by desires, has the spirit of renunciation, and is not perplexed by dualities, is unbound, and he moves towards liberation.
>
> It is simple ignorance to differentiate between renunciation and practice of action. Renunciation involves renouncing fruits of action and not action as such.
>
> One may become liberated by renouncing action as well as by engaging in it. The truth of the matter is that the two are the two sides of the same coin. *Renouncing* is renouncing fruits of action; and it is not inaction.
>
> However, renunciation is not easy without action.

By engaging in *karma-yoga*, one attains the state of freedom.

Actions do not bind one who has his senses under control and has self-mastery, behaves ethically, and sees his self in others.

The person who realizes the divinity within and becomes aware of the truth understands that he is not involved in all his activities such as sensing, walking, sleeping, and breathing.

It is the senses that interact with their objects.

Just as a lotus leaf in the pond is not covered by water and stays aloof, so an unattached person devoted to God is not touched by evil.

The *karma-yogin* performs his duties without any attachment, only for the sake of self-purification.

The *yogin* without attachment to the fruits of action achieves well-deserved peace of mind, whereas the person untouched by his divinity and prompted by desire and cravings is bound to the world, unhappy, and not liberated.

The person who is able to overcome the fluctuations of the mind lives peacefully without influencing or getting influenced, by his nine sensory outlets, viz. the two ears, the two eyes, the two nostrils, and the mouth along with the organs of excretion and procreation.

The real *self* within is neither the creator nor the doer; and does not relate to the fruits of one's action. What we found happening are functions of nature and not of the *self*.

Sin and virtue are not the attributes of the *self*. Lacking this wisdom, ignorant people are perplexed and confused.

As the shining sun dispels all darkness, the knowledge of one's true being lights up the true *self*.

Focused on the *self*, devoted to its knowing, and becoming aware of it, people reach the state of wisdom from which there is no fall. All the sins washed away, they become liberated and become self-actualized persons.

Self-actualized persons look at other people with or without knowledge, or a cow, an elephant, a dog or even a dog-eater with equanimity because they realize that what sustains them is the *Self*, which they all share.

With such equanimity and finding no flaw to blame others, people become unbound and get liberated from the cycle of birth and death.

Those with an equanimous mind, even embodied, can become self-actualized persons, because they realize that they share the same *Self*.

One who does not rejoice when he encounters pleasures or become depressed in the face of the unpleasant and has right knowledge and therefore is not puzzled, perplexed, or confused achieves self-actualization.

When the mind overcomes attachment and is not attracted by external things, it finds peace and happiness inherent in the *self*. Such self-controlled persons realize their inherent divinity.

> Pleasures obtained by sense-object contact are sources of sorrow that bind men to the world. No wise person is happy in that situation.
>
> He who is able to control his desires and overcomes anger becomes a *yogin*. While embodied he enjoys lasting peace and happiness.
>
> With such inner peace and happiness, and enlightened, a *yogin* achieves divinity and becomes a self-actualized self.
>
> The virtuous men with their sins vanquished, doubts cleared, minds focused find their happiness in the well-being of all.
>
> Such people, who are free from desire and anger, have controlled the wanderings of their mind and stay focused on the knowledge of the *self*, become self-actualized persons.
>
> The one, who shuts out the sense-object contact, focuses on the middle of his eyebrows, controls his breath, senses and the mind, abandons his desires, and is free from fear and anger, finds himself free and liberated.
>
> Knowing that divinity lies in service, one therefore should perform his duties and find peace for himself.

The central point of paramount significance conveyed by these verses is that what is necessary is not renunciation of action, but renunciation in action. The latter involves paying as little attention to the consequences when an ethically bound person performs his actions.

6

Yoga and Meditation

KRISHNA continues his gospel:

The one who performs his duties without hankering for fruits is a true renouncer of action. He is a true *yogin*, and not the one of inaction who abstains from daily activities. *Sanyasa* is not giving up work, but engaging in it without selfishness.

Renunciation is a disciplined action; it is not anarchy. It consists in developing a well-controlled, regulated, and unselfish mind.

Work is the way to reach the pinnacle of *yoga*. The person who scaled the peak, achieves serenity and tranquillity of the mind.

When a person detached from sensory indulgence ceases to be swayed by the wanderings of the mind, he is considered as the one who has scaled the heights of *yoga*.

Rise above selfishness, Oh Arjuna, by discarding the ego and finding yourself in the true *self*. The ego-driven *self* is the foe while the self free from the ego is the friend.

Subdued, ego becomes the friend; unsubdued, it is one's enemy.

When a person conquers the ego and gains self-control, he realizes the Divine in his self, finds peace and becomes indifferent to such dualities as heat and cold, pleasure and pain, honour and dishonour.

The practising *yogin* who is content with what he knows and does, is unwavering in his mind and indifferent to what comes on the way, cold, stone or gold.

He looks at people with equanimity whether they are friends, foes or indifferent persons, whether they like him or hate him, whether they are saints or sinners.

Remaining aloof, self-restrained, and free from desires and longing for possessions, the *yogin* focuses his mind on the unchanging, true *self.*

He situates himself at a clean and comfortable place, which is neither too high nor too low, and is covered with cloth or hide or sacred grass.

Sitting in that place, the *yoga* practitioner with his mind steady and focused, and controlling his senses attempts to purify himself.

He holds his neck erect and the rest of the body steady and fixes his gaze on the tip of his nose without looking around.

With his mind calm without any fear, he focuses his thoughts on the Divine.

Engaged in such practices relentlessly with a controlled and steady mind, the *yogin* finds peace and moves towards self-actualization.

A *yogin* does not fast, nor does he overeat. He does not sleep too much or stay awake all the time.

He who is not moderate in his habits, whether in eating or procreation, sleeping or waking cannot practise *yoga* well.

With the mind steady and disciplined, free from all ego involvement, the *yogin* becomes an integrated person and moves towards self-actualization.

Like the candle which burns without flickering when there is no wind disturbing it, the *yogin* who subdues his wandering thoughts focuses on the self unmitigated by blowing thoughts.

In a yogic state, the mind is still and restrained by the practice of concentration. Then the individual *self* finds its unity in the universal *Self*; and rejoices in it.

Independent of the senses, the steadfast mind may grasp the boundless and unending happiness, and get closer to the Truth.

Knowing that Truth, the *yogin* realizes that there is nothing more important. He would not suffer from any grievous pain.

The person who practises *yoga* with determination and focused mind breaks his link with suffering and becomes undisturbed.

The detached person, whose mind is focused on knowing the truth, who works to render service, he is unbound by *karma* and the consequences of his action.

He abandons all ego-involved desires, restrains the mind and controls the senses from all angles.

With absolute focus, he anchors his mind in the *self*, thinking of nothing else. He moves step by step closer to his goal of achieving peace and freedom.

He restrains whatsoever causes his mind to wander and brings it back to focus on the *self.*

When the *yogin* has a peaceful mind, puts his passions and sins away and purifies his *self*, he reaches a state of self-realization.

The sinless *yogin* is an integrated person who enjoys peace and happiness and becomes self-actualized.

Such an integrated person with his mind attuned to *yoga*, sees his self in other beings, and others in himself.

He sees divinity in all beings and realizes divinity and unity among others. He sees them in himself.

Whatever his mode of living, such an integrated *yogin* leads a divine life.

The one, who thus realizes the pervasiveness of divinity across all beings and feels their pleasures and pains as his own, is considered a true *yogin.*

Arjuna observed:

The *yoga* you explained is about having equanimity of mind. However, I find myself restless, unable to keep my mind steady and firmly grounded.

The mind wavers, impetuous, strong, and stubborn. I believe, it is difficult to control, like the wind.

Krishna's response:

Yes, it is true, the mind is restless and difficult to restrain. Nevertheless, it can be controlled.

Yogic state is difficult to reach without self-control and without pursuing the right means.

Arjuna went on to ask:

What is the way to go, Oh Krishna, for the one who cannot control his mind and practise *yoga*, though he has the faith and intention to bring his mind under control?

What is the fate of the one whose mind drifts like a passing cloud, puzzled and without a firm foothold?

Having failed in action, confused, and unable to control his mind and realize his self, would he not disappear like the dispersed cloud?

Oh Krishna, pray, dispel this doubt. Only you can help.

Krishna answers:

For the one who renders service and follows his duties, there is no grief in this world or thereafter.

A person who led a virtuous life for many years, but slipped from the yogic path is born again into a prosperous and virtuous household.

Alternatively, he may be born into a family of wise men following the yogic path.

Thereby he regains the images of divinity he had in the previous life and starts again moving further towards self-actualization.

He moves forward irresistibly seeking knowledge of *yoga* even beyond what is contained in the Vedas.

The *yogin* who assiduously engages himself in the pursuit of freedom improving from birth to birth, finally achieves self-realization and becomes a self-actualized person.

Such a *yogin* is superior to the one who renounces his actions and becomes an ascetic, better than the so-called wise men adept in spiritual learning; and clearly greater than the one who merely performs the rituals. So, Oh Arjuna, I urge you to become a *yogin* and act.

Even among the *yogins* the self-realized person is the one who with full faith in the Divine immerses his self in the Divine.

This chapter further elaborates on what is implied in the assertion of the significance of renunciation in action, as distinguished from renunciation *of* action. In this context of psychological counselling, a successful therapist provides a theoretical structure from which the advice springs, so that it does not sound to the client arbitrary and ad hoc. Such counselling will be more persuasive for performing positive action.

7

Yoga for Self-Actualization

KRISHNA continues his counsel:

By practising *yoga* with a spiritual bent of mind, you will understand without any doubt what divinity means.

I will now explain to you what self-realization is, by understanding which you will have nothing more to learn.

Only one among many thousands who strive to achieve divinity really succeeds.

The earth, water, fire, air, space, mind, understanding, and the ego sense are in my eightfold physical nature.

However, my higher nature by which the world is sustained is different.

The world displays both aspects of my dual nature. However, I am the one who creates, sustains, and dissolves it.

I am the string that runs through a cluster of gems. There is nothing beyond me.

I am the source of all, whether it is the taste in the waters, shine in the moon, or the light of the sun. I am the manliness in men, the sound carried by the air, and the essence of the sacred syllable *om* in the Vedas.

I am in the odour of the earth, the brightness in the fire. Indeed I am the life that sustains all existence. You find me in the piousness of the ascetics.

Understand, Oh Arjuna, I am the everlasting seed that generates all beings. I am the wisdom among the wise, the splendour that underlies all wonderful things.

Beyond being the seed that generates all beings, I am the wisdom behind intellect; and I am the splendour of splendours.

I am the strength of the mighty without any attachment. However, I have the insatiable appetite for righteousness.

Whatever the state of one's being - integrated, passionate, or indolent - all these *gunas* (qualities) emanate from me; but I am not in them, they are in me.

Deluded by the three *gunas*, men do not recognize me who is the imperishable beyond all the qualities of nature.

This delusion (*maya*) generated by me is difficult to overcome. However, those who find their refuge in the Divine will succeed in dispelling the *maya*.

Those engaged in evil acts, foolish, downgraded on human scale, and carried away by the illusiveness of the world are devilish. They do not seek refuge in me.

There are four kinds of virtuous men who worship God. They include men in distress, knowledge seekers, people who are after wealth and finally those with wisdom.

Of all of them, the people with wisdom single-mindedly participate in the Divine. So they are exceedingly intimate with me. I am dear to them and they are dear to me.

All the four kinds of people are indeed noble persons. However, the men of wisdom are especially dear to me. They are well integrated persons; and have me as their most sought-after goal.

After going through the cycle of birth and death, they finally find me as the Supreme and all that there is. Such men are not many.

On the other side, those men with minds biased by desires, constrained by their limitations, resort to worshipping all kinds of gods and performing all kinds of rituals and ceremonies.

Without regard to the mode of worship or form of the worshipping deity, I help them to do so in an unswerving and steadfast manner.

With faith in divinity by performing any of these forms of worship, the seeker fulfils the objects of his desire; because I myself so decreed.

However, the benefits gained by these men of less foresight are temporary. Such worshippers of gods go to those gods. My devotees come to me.

Men without proper understanding of me, and not aware of my high nature, changeless and sovereign, who is essentially unmanifest, think of me as manifest.

People deluded by my magical creation (*maya*) do not realize that I have neither a beginning nor an end. I am not revealed to them.

I know the beings that lived in the past, living in the present, and that will live in the future; and who come to me; but they do not know me.

Those people deluded by dualities born by attachment and repulsion are confused and fail to grasp the truth.

However, those men who overcome sin by virtuous deeds, and are free from the delusion of dualities, worship me devotedly sticking to their resolve.

Believing in me, they find relief from old age and death, realize all about the self and render selfless service.

Those who know I am the one who governs material and spiritual realms and make their offerings with an integrated mind realize me, even if it is at the end of their life in this world.

This chapter asserts again the significance of the authenticity of the therapist, his credentials and the need to instill confidence in the client that he is dealing with a person who can be trusted. Trust of the client in the competence of the counsellor is a necessary condition for the success of psychotherapy.

8

Yoga of Concentration

The Nature of the Absolute Sustaining All Existence and the Way of Action for Self-Actualization

THERE was much food for Arjuna's thought in Krishna's gospel as given in the previous chapter. As a consequence, a number of relevant questions perplexed Arjuna's mind. So he went on to ask Krishna:

> What is the Absolute, the so-called *Brahman*? What indeed is the *self*? What actually is meant by action? What is the domain of the spiritual distinguished from the material realm? Wherein do the gods dwell?
>
> What is the *karma* that drives the body? And how does it engage in it? Again, tell me how the self-controlled person may realize divinity as he leaves this world?

Krishna addresses the above questions in the following way:

> *Brahman*, the Absolute, is that which is imperishable and supreme. It stands at the peak of all existence. The self is the spiritual component of being. *Karma* is what precipitates and brings into being the manifest world.
>
> Change is inherent in all the created material things. Cosmic spirit runs through all spiritual manifestations. The body is the necessary instrument of action that causes change.

There can be no doubt that the one who at the time of death is thinking of and focusing on me becomes one with me.

Whatever one thinks at the time of his death, he later becomes. Thus, the present birth lays the seeds for future births.

Therefore, remembering me at all times, go on and fight. By concentrating on me and focusing your mind on wisdom get rid of all doubts. You shall attain divinity.

With a steadfast and unwandering mind and gaining proficiency in *yoga* by continuous practice, one participates in the Divine and reaches the supreme goal.

He who meditates on that which sustains the universe, the subtle and imponderable, and which dispels all darkness; and he who at the time of death, with faith in the power of *yoga* focusing his vital energies between eyebrows remembers the past attains divinity.

I shall presently describe to you that imperishable state which the Vedic seers without attachment have sought for gaining self-control.

With the senses restrained and the mind concentrated on the heart, the *yogin* focuses on the vital energies in the head and continues to practise meditation.

Chanting the mystical syllable *om*, which represents the *Brahman*, remembering the divinity, the one who leaves the body moves closer to the supreme goal he is seeking.

With the steadfast focus of mind and meditating on the spiritual, he reaches the divine state.

With the realization of his spiritual side, one breaks the cycle of birth and death and transcends the ephemeral world of sorrow and suffering. He reaches the best possible state of perfection.

From the highest world of *Brahman* to the mundane and ordinary, all beings are subject to the cycle of birth and death. However, for the one who finds the supreme and reaches the divine state, there is no return from it.

In the world of the *Brahman*, a day lasts for ages; so does the night.

At the dawn of the day, life begins to manifest; and while the nights sets in, it becomes unmanifest and loses its identity.

Various forms of life that arise during the day get dissolved at night and are born again at day-break.

Beyond the unmanifest, however, there is the primordial state, which is everlasting and does not perish with others.

Such primordial state is indestructible. It is the supreme state. And those who reach that state find their permanent abode there. Having reached that divine state, there is no return.

By unwavering devotion one may reach the supreme state, which is the source of all-pervading existence.

Now, Arjuna, let me explain to you which of the

departing *yogins* are reborn and those who are not born again.

The people who die during the six months when the sun moves northward on the day filled with bright light with the *Brahman* in mind are not reborn.

Those who leave their body during dark nights when the sun is on the southern course are reborn.

We have two courses one of the light and the other of darkness. The one who takes the path of light does not return to the world. The one who takes the other course is reborn.

Being aware of these courses, the *yogin* is not deluded. Therefore, Arjuna, commit yourself firmly to the course of light.

Knowing all this, perform your duties without hankering after fruits. By good actions, through service, proper offerings and also by learning of the Vedas, the *yogin* becomes a self-actualized person.

Here is a mix of mythology and practical suggestions for focusing attention on the required action. It is a blend of theory and practice. It is necessary to let the client become aware of the roots of his tradition and how the suggested course of action is consistent with it. It is important to emphasize the cultivation of right habits for performing one's duties.

9

Raja-Yoga : The Royal Way to Self-Actualization

To you, who do not entertain petty objections, I will reveal the profound secret of ultimate wisdom, the knowledge of which would make you immune to all sins.

Such knowledge is supreme, has the highest sanctity of law. It is imperishable and easy to gain.

People who do not realize this truth will not become self-realized and find the divinity they seek. They are born again into the world of things and desire.

I am all-pervasive in my unmanifest form. All things find their being in me; but I do not dwell in them.

Beings do not exist in me; but I bring them into existence and sustain them.

Just as the ever moving air subsists in space unending, so do all beings exist within me.

At the end of the cycle of existence, all beings move back to me. At the beginning of another cycle, I release them.

They start all over, become part of nature (*prakriti*), and play their roles.

All my actions do not bind me because I am unattached and indifferent to the outcome of my actions.

Guided by me, nature gives birth to all things, mobile and immobile. Thus it manifests in manifold ways; the wheel of the world keeps moving.

Embodied, unwise people deride me as another incarnated man. They are unaware of my transcendental nature, and that I am the real source of all manifestation.

By partaking in the evil nature of devils and demons, their desires, thoughts and action, they become futile and mindless.

However, noble people with capable minds resort to their divine nature. They are focused on the divinity knowing that it is the imperishable source of all being.

With unceasing praise and admiration for and faith in the Divine, they steadfastly strive to achieve divinity.

Again, some others giving up even knowledge seek me as one with them or different from them or in manifold other ways, finding me everywhere.

I am the object of all rituals, service, and offerings made to the Divine. I am the healing in the medicinal herb. I am the sacred hymn. I am ghee and fire in the oblation.

I am the father, the mother, and the grandfather, the supporter and the sustainer of this world. I am in the sacred object of knowledge, the holy syllable *om* in the *Rig*, the *Sama*, and the *Yajus* as well.

I am the fruit as well as the doer of action. I am witness to what happens and what does not happen. I give refuge to the suffering. I am a friend who helps without expecting anything in return. I am the source of the origin and the dissolution of the world. I am the indestructible seed behind all that sprouts, and the treasure of all fruits of action.

Oh Arjuna, I generate heat; I make it rain and stop the rain. I cause death; and I am behind immortality. I am being; and also non-being.

People who study the Vedas, drink *soma* (juice) are relieved of their sins. Worshipping me with all kinds of offerings they seek to reach heaven. They indeed will go to heaven and enjoy the pleasures of gods.

After enjoying the heavenly comforts, they are emptied of the good they had done, they are back in the world of mortals. Thus in accordance with the Vedic laws they become subject to birth and death.

To my devotees who incessantly meditate on and worship me, I grant them prosperity and safety.

Even those who worship other gods with faith, they also serve me, Arjuna, even though it is not strictly in accordance with true laws.

It is because I am the enjoyer of all their offerings. If they do not recognize this, they fail to reach the goal of liberation.

Worshippers of gods go to gods; and worshippers of the devils to the devils. Those who serve the spirits go to the spirits; and those who serve the Divine become Divine.

I accept whatever people with devotion and with pure heart offer me, whether it is a leaf, a flower, a fruit, or water.

> Oh Arjuna, whatever you do, eat, or give away, or service you perform, let it be in the name of the Divine.
>
> That indeed is the way to be unbound by good or evil built into one's actions.
>
> Divinity is the same in all beings without regard to their standing at a given time. Divinity is pervasive and not confined to this person or that.
>
> Even the most vicious man, if he single-mindedly dedicates himself to the Divine, should be considered virtuous, because he is on the right path.
>
> He quickly becomes a righteous person and enjoys everlasting peace.
>
> Those who seek divinity, find their salvation and become unbound without regard to the caste they are born into, whether they are men or women.
>
> Realize how much easier it would be for the sages and those born into sacred families to reach the state of liberation.
>
> Fixing the mind on divinity with devotion and reverence, the one who seeks divinity becomes Divine.

This chapter succinctly summarizes the path of *raja-yoga*, the nature of and royal route to realize the Divine inherent in each person. It emphasizes the ethical aspect of action, the criteria of proper worship, and the means of cultivating right conduct.

10

Limitless Manifestations of the Divine Spirit

KRISHNA continues his counsel:

Let me once again tell you with your good in mind and for your benefit what is supreme in life. You may take delight in knowing it.

Neither the pantheon of gods, nor the great seers are aware of my origin because I am their source and of that exists.

He who realizes that the divinity in me is transcendent, unborn and has no beginning, overcomes ignorance and becomes free. Ignorance is the root cause of delusions and sins.

Intelligence, knowledge, non-delusion, patience, truthfulness, self-control, equal mindedness in pleasure as well as in pain, being and non-being, fear and courage, nonviolence, equanimity, contentment, self-discipline, fame or notoriety are the different states of the mind that emanate from me.

The seven great seers of the bygone age, the four Manus and all the creatures of the world and their progeny are my mental creations and partake in my nature.

Those who engage themselves in *yoga* will have a

steady and integrated mind. There can be no doubt about this.

All things have their origin in the divinity; they manifest from me. Endowed with this conviction, wise people worship me.

Their thoughts are centred around me and their lives are devoted to me. Being with me and conversing with me, they are content and joyful.

To them, who are continually devoted to me and worship me with love, I enable them to focus their mind and become Divine and be a part of me.

With compassion for those who are devoted to divinity, I dispel the darkness of ignorance and kindle the light of wisdom.

In the divine state, the light of wisdom shines, dispelling the darkness of ignorance.

Arjuna says:

Krishna, you are the Supreme, primordial God, pervasive without a beginning or end. You are the abode of highest values. Your lasting divine spirit sanctifies everything.

You are so hailed by all the sages such as Narada, Asita, Devala, and Vyasa. Now, you yourself declare it to me.

I consider everything you tell me as true. Neither the gods nor the devils know your origin and manifestations.

You are the Supreme Spirit, the cause, and commander of all manifestations. You alone know the true *Self* as yourself, God of gods.

You should reveal to me your divine manifestations without any exception by which you pervade and dwell in this world and beyond.

How may I know you, Oh *Yogin*? On what objects do I meditate to realize you?

Oh Krishna, tell me once again at length your yogic abilities and powers. I am not satiated by the taste of the nectar of your words.

Krishna responds:

Okay, I will inform you of my Divine forms, but only the prominent ones among them because there is no end to them.

Arjuna, I am centred in the hearts of all creatures. I am the beginning, the middle, and the end of all that lives.

Among the Vedic gods, I am Vishnu; among the luminaries I am the radiant sun. I am Marichi of the storm gods; and I am moon among the stars.

Among the Vedas, I am the *Samaveda*. Of the heavenly Lords, I am Indra. Among the senses, I am the mind; and I am consciousness in beings.

Among the eleven Rudras I am Siva. Among Yakshas and Rakshasas, I am Kubera, the lord of wealth. Among the eight Vasus I am Agni (fire). I am Meru among mountain peaks.

The intellectuals know me as Brihaspathi. The heroes of war consider me as Skanda. I am the sea among the lakes.

Among the great sages I am Bhrigu; among the letters

I am the *om*. I am the silent prayer in meditation. I am as immovable as the Himalayas.

I am the sacred fig among the trees, and I am Narada among the divine seers. Among the musicians, I am the one named Chitraratha. I am Kapila among the great sages.

Among horses, I am considered Uccaihsravah born out of sea when it was churned for *amrita*. Among the great elephants, I am Airavata; and among humans I am their ruler.

I am the thunderbolt (the weapon used by Indra) among weapons. I am the wish granting cow. I am the god of love among progenitors; and among serpents I am Vasuki.

Among the mighty snakes I am Ananta; I am Varuna among the creatures of water. Among the departed ancestors, I am Aryama. I am the Yama who maintains law and order in the universe.

Among those of demon ancestry, I am Prahlada. Among those who count, I am time. I am lion, king of all beasts; and I am Garuda among birds.

I am the wind that purifies. As a warrior, I am Rama. Among creatures of water, I am the alligator. I am the Ganga among rivers.

I am the beginning and end of the universe. I am also in the middle of it all. Among the sciences, I am the one that investigates the *self*. I am the dialectic behind all logical discussions.

Among the letters of the alphabet, I am the first letter

"a". I am the duality in grammatical compounds. I transcend time. I am the one who dispenses justice from all sides.

I am the past, the present, and the things to come. In the feminine, I am the fame, glory, speech, memory, intelligence, endurance, and patience.

Also, I am Brihatsaman, the most glorious melody in the *Samaveda*. Among the Vedic *mantras*, I am the Gayatri. I am Margashirsha among the months. Of the seasons, I am the spring.

For the gamblers who cheat in the game, I am the dice. I am the strength of the valiant. I am the glory of the victorious; and I am the virtue among the virtuous.

Among Yadavas, I am Vasudeva. I am Arjuna among Pandavas. Among the great sages, I am Vyasa. Among the men of foresight, I am the seer Shukra.

I am the rod to chastise; I am the wise planning behind those succeed. I am the silence behind all well-kept secrets; and I am wisdom underlying knowledge.

Moreover, I am the seed that generates all existing things. Nothing, whether moving or standing, exists without me.

My divine manifestations are endless. What I have said to you, Arjuna, are just examples of my infinite glory.

All beings that have energy, power, and enjoy glory are but a fragment of my many-sided splendour.

What is the need for you, Arjuna, to have such detailed knowledge? I sustain the entire universe with just a fraction of my power.

Once again, Krishna explains the nature of divinity He represents, which is present in all beings, but manifests in different forms. Its relevance to counselling in general is to help to relieve the client of any guilt feelings that may be troubling him by suggesting that underlying all actions, there are hidden persuaders which go beyond one's intention and one's personal responsibilities.

11

Vision of Lord's Cosmic Form

ARJUNA says:

Your discourse on the *Self* to bless me is both magical and spiritual. I have now overcome my delusions.

You have enlightened me on the origin and dissolution of all beings as well as about your eternal splendour.

Oh Supreme Being! The Highest Spirit! You have described yourself in such detail. However, I would like to see with my own eyes the infinite and glorious form of yours.

If you think it proper, Oh great *yogin*, reveal to me your changeless, eternal *Self.*

Krishna responds:

Look now, Arjuna, at my hundredfold, no, thousandfold divine forms of different hues and shapes.

See the twelve Adityas, the eight Vasus, the eleven Rudras, the two Ashvins, and the seven types of Maruts, Arjuna, the forms that were not seen until now by anyone.

Today, you see existing within me the entire universe, whether changing or still, and any other things you may wish to see.

However, you cannot see me with your human eye. I

now endow you with supernatural vision; so you may become aware of my divine power.

Sanjaya continues his narration to Dhritarashtra:

Saying these words, Krishna, the great *yogin*, revealed to Arjuna his transcendent, Divine form.

With several mouths and eyes, many marvellous things, divine ornaments, and armaments.

Wearing divine garlands and garments of limitless splendour with wonderful fragrance, and great illumination, resembling the rays of a thousand suns lighting up the sky.

See, Arjuna, the entire universe unfolding. I am the God of gods.

His hair-standing, the amazed Arjuna bowed with his head bent and hands folded.

Arjuna says:

In your body, Krishna, I see all gods, various forms of beings in existence, the Brahma, the creator sitting on the lotus throne. I see all the sages and the celestial snakes.

I see you with many hands, bellies, faces and eyes, your infinite form spread in all directions. Oh Lord of the universe, I see no beginning, no middle, and no end to your manifold manifestations.

I see your crown, armour, discus, and a mass of dazzling and immeasurable light and the glowing radiance of fire and the blazing sun.

You are the ever-present Supreme to be realized. You

are the foundational ground of the universe. I believe, you are the endless guardian of the eternal law. You are indeed the Primordial Person.

I realize that you have no beginning or end or something in the middle. You are endowed with infinite power and countless arms. The sun and the moon are your eyes. Your face is a raging fire, which could burn up the entire universe.

You pervade the entire space from heaven to earth. You are all over. When your wondrous and terrifying form is seen, all the three worlds tremble.

Indeed, many gods join you. Some worship you with folded hands. Groups of great sages and perfect beings hail and worship you with sacred hymns.

The Rudras, the Adityas, the Vasus, and the less perfect persons, Vishvedevas, the two Ashvins, the Maruts and the ancestral spirits, *gandharvas*, *yakshas*, demons, and the liberated ones look at you with amazement.

Looking at your transcendental form of several mouths, many eyes, your mighty armour, huge thighs and feet, many bellies and the many terrible, protruding tusks, the worlds shake; and so do I.

Oh Vishnu! When I see you as high as the sky, radiating many splendours, with your mouth wide open, your large eyes glowing, I tremble with fear unable to stand steady and be peaceful.

When I see your mouth with those frightening teeth glowing like all-consuming fire at the dissolution of the world, I become unsteady and restless. Be gracious, Krishna, the God of gods in whom the world takes refuge.

All those sons of Dhritarashtra along with hosts of kings, Bhishma, Drona, Karna, and also the great warriors from our side, are rushing into your awesome mouths with their terrifying teeth, some caught between the teeth and their heads crushed.

Like the fast moving streams of water in the rivers rushing to the sea, the so-called heroes in the world enter into your blazing mouth.

Just like the moths entering into the glittering fire perish in it, these men rushing into your mouth meet their destruction.

Gobbling up and licking from all sides with your mouths full of fire, you search the world with the dreadful radiation of your luminous energy.

I salute you, the God of gods; tell me graciously who you really are with this awesome form. I long to know the nature of the activity of your primordial being, which I do not quite understand.

Krishna responds:

I am the all-powerful time causing the dissolution of the world. Here, now, I am engaged in the worlds into me. Even without you, these fighters in the two opposing camps will cease to exist.

Therefore, stand up and win glory. Conquering your enemies, enjoy this kingdom of plenty. I have already ended their life. You are just a show, an occasion.

Go on, kill Drona, Bhishma, Jayadratha, Karna, and other warriors poised against you. They are already doomed by me.

Sanjaya continues his narration to Dhritarashtra:

Arjuna heard what Krishna said. Nervous, trembling with folded hands falling at Krishna's feet, Arjuna spoke to Krishna in a faltering voice:

It is indeed very appropriate that the world rejoices and finds delight in glorifying you. The demons are terrified and flee with fear in all directions; and the learned men adore you in admiration.

It is only proper they salute you. You are the exalted one greater than the creator himself, Brahma. You embody the infinite being; and the God of gods. The world finds its refuge in you. You stand for being and non-being, and go even beyond.

You are the primal God in whom the world rests. You are knower as well as all that is to be known. You are the supreme goal, transcendental abode. Your form is infinite and unbound.

You are the pervasive wind (Vayu) and the Lord of destruction (Yama); you are the substance-sustaining fire as well as water. You are the shining moon and the presiding deity of all creatures. You are Prajapati, the predecessor of all great men. I salute you a thousand times; I hail you repeatedly.

I salute you from the front, behind, and every side. You have unlimited power and immeasurable strength. You penetrate everything; and therefore you are all there is.

Taking you as my companion and unaware of your greatness I rushed to you hastily and thoughtlessly addressed you simply as Krishna. I have treated you unceremoniously, privately and in public while taking rest, sitting, eating, or playing games. I beg you to forgive me, you are the inestimable Lord.

You are the progenitor of all beings in the world, whether moving or standing. You are the supreme teacher worthy of worship. You are unparalleled; no one is equal to you with your incomparable might.

Therefore, let me salute and prostrate at your feet and beg your forgiveness. You should grant this as the father to his son, as a comrade to a friend, and a lover to the beloved.

I have seen what I never saw before. I rejoice in seeing what I never saw before; but I am shaken with fear.

Oh Lord, I wish to see you in the familiar form. Be gracious and grant my request.

Krishna takes his human form saying:

With my yogic powers and in an obliging mood, I revealed to you my supreme, cosmic form, primordial and infinite, which no one but you have ever seen.

No one by studying Vedas, making sacrifices, offering gifts, or observing austerities has ever seen me in this form, except you.

You need not be afraid or confused seeing my transcendental form. Free from fear, you may now see my other form.

Sanjaya continues to describe the battle scene:

> After so speaking to Arjuna, Krishna took on the usual form, thus consoling the terror-stricken Arjuna.
>
> Arjuna, then, seeing Krishna in the familiar form regained his equanimity and gained his normal composure.

Krishna says to Arjuna:

> My Divine form you have seen is something that even gods constantly crave to see.
>
> I may not be seen as you have even by those who study the Vedas, observe austerities, or make all kinds of offerings to me.
>
> I can be truthfully seen only by persons with complete and focused devotion. That is my nature.
>
> The one who carries out his activities without attachment or aversion to other beings and with the devoted goal of reaching the Divine becomes the self-actualized person.

The above verses describe in addition how a person may reach a state of self-actualization. The emphasis is on right intentions, proper worship and righteous conduct as the necessary attributes for achieving self-actualization.

12

Bhakti-Yoga : Devotional Path Towards Self-Actualization

Arjuna asks Krishna:

> You have mentioned about your devotees who contemplate on the Absolute Unmanifested *Brahman*, and also those who worship you. Which of them know the *yoga* best?

Krishna responds:

> Those who worship with complete concentration and have full of faith in me are the ones I consider to be perfect in *yoga*. They are the self-actualized persons. (Krishna thus makes it very clear that worship of personalized god is preferable to meditating on the Absolute.)
>
> However, those who contemplate on the unmanifest and undefinable Absolute, restraining their senses, maintaining equanimity of mind, taking delight in the happiness of others, also reach divinity.
>
> It is difficult to focus on and realize the unmanifest Absolute.
>
> However, those who with full faith, necessary concentration, and due devotion meditate on the Divine are straightway saved from the ocean of death-bound existence.

So, focus your mind and concentrate on the Divine backed by proper understanding. There is no doubt then, that you become a part of the Divine.

If, however, you have difficulty to focus your thoughts steadfast on divinity, then engage yourself in practices of concentration.

If you cannot concentrate your mind by practice, then you aim at rendering service for self-actualization.

In case, when even this is not possible, engage in disciplined, selfless action without craving for any fruits of such actions.

Knowing is better than mere doing; meditation is better than simply knowing. Renunciation of fruits of action is even superior to meditation because such renunciation results at once in peace of mind.

That person is dear to me who has no hatred towards other being, who is loving, compassionate and unselfish, balanced when faced with pain or pleasure, and patient in enduring suffering.

Who is ever happy and content, self-disciplined with steadfast determination, his mind and intellect committed to me, a true devotee of mine is indeed dear to me.

He who neither belittles or is belittled by the world, who is not elated or anguished and free from conflicts is also dear to me.

The person with pure heart and no expectation of any reward, diligent in action, unattached, and untroubled and does not get lost in daydreams is dear to me.

> I am fond of the one who is devoted to me giving up his grief and desires, and is beyond good and evil.
>
> He is equanimous when with a friend or foe, when he faces honour or dishonour, cold or heat, pleasure or pain because he has no attachment.
>
> He feels the same facing praise or blame. He silently accepts whatever comes his way. He is steadfast with no abode of his own. Such a devoted person is dear to me.
>
> Those devotees of mine who develop such lasting virtues with full faith in me as the Supreme Person, they are truly dear to me.

The above verses outline the nature of devotion and how one may cultivate the mindset required for proper devotion. Further, they reinforce the need to have undiluted devotion and faith in the healer.

13

Karma-Yoga and Nature of the Subject and the Object

ARJUNA asks Krishna to tell him about the field of objects (*prakriti*) and the knowing spirit (*purusha*).

> The body stands for the object of knowledge, and the one who becomes aware of it is the knower.
>
> I am the ground of the object as well as its knower.
>
> I now describe to you briefly what the ground/field is, its manifestations, and who the knower of the field is and what his powers are.
>
> It has been the subject of many hymns chanted by sages in several distinct ways. We find well-reasoned and definitive statements about them in the *Brahmasutras*.
>
> The five gross elements in the material world, the ego, the intellect as well as the unmanifest, the ten senses, and the five objects of the senses,
>
> attachment and aversion, pleasure and pain, the physical organism, and the sustaining intellect are the field and its multifarious manifestations;
>
> absence of pride and deceit, nonviolence, endurance, righteousness, serving the teacher, cleanliness of body and mind, steadfastness, and self-control;

non-indulgence in the objects of senses, egolessness, knowing the evils of birth, death, old age, sickness, and pain;

detachment, excessive affection for children, unfailing equanimity in the face of pleasant as well as unpleasant,

with complete attention, unwavering devotion to the Divine, sitting in uncrowded solitary places,

relentlessly pursuing spiritual knowledge gaining insights into true knowledge, and knowing without any confusion how it is different from the false.

I will now explain to you what one should know, by knowing which he gains the supreme knowledge of the Absolute, the *Brahman*, who is without a beginning and transcends the very notion of existence, and thus becomes a self-actualized person.

The *Brahman* is all-pervasive and contains the entire universe within his fold. With hands and feet everywhere, eyes and ears seeing and hearing from all angles, he dwells in and envelops all existence.

He manifests all sensory qualities without having the senses. He is detached from all the dispositions of the nature (*prakriti*); and yet enjoys all the sensory qualities.

He is within and outside of all beings. He is moving as well as unmoving. He is too elusive to be known; far away and yet so near.

He is an indivisible whole; and yet has the appearance of being divided.

He is the light behind all lights; and transcends all kinds of darkness. He is accessible through knowledge; because he is entrenched within each person.

Thus, he is the field, the objects in it, and the knowledge of them, as I briefly described. Now, my devotees are fit to grasp that knowledge.

The material universe (*prakriti*) as well as the immaterial self (*purusha*) are without any beginning. All modes and physical forms that are manifest in the world are the products of *prakriti.*

Prakriti is said to be the material cause of the universe; and *purusha* is behind one's experience of pain and pleasure.

Purusha embodied in *prakriti* has the experience of all modes and manifest forms of the latter. Attachment to such experiences binds one to the consequent births with good or evil dispositions.

The *purusha*, the embodied spirit, is considered to be the witness, the one who permits, supports, and sustains; and therefore he is the Lord in one's physical frame.

The actions of the person with true understanding of *purusha* and *prakriti* and its manifestations do not bind him or stand in the way of his liberation.

One may become a self-actualized person through meditation, or by knowledge or by actions without attachment.

However, some people, not knowing these three ways of *yoga*, hearing about it from others, engage in worship. They also transcend the cycle of births by such devotion.

Whatever exists, whether moving or standing, arises out of the union of the subject and the object, the knower and the known.

The one, who becomes aware of the fact that all beings emanate from the same source which does not perish when its manifestations disappear, knows the truth.

It is because he who sees that the same *self* is shared by all becomes free from the delusions of the ego and moves toward self-actualization.

He who knows that all actions emanate from *prakriti* and that *purusha* is not the doer has the true knowledge.

When one realizes that the manifest multiplicity of things have their origin in a single source he becomes a self-actualized person.

The spirit (*purusha*) is indestructible because it has no beginning and is without any qualities. Though it finds its abode in the body, it is not the agent of actions and consequently not tainted by them.

Just as the all-pervading space is not tainted, because of its subtlety, so the embodied self (*purusha*) is not stained.

Just like the sun who lights up the entire world, so does the subject illumine the objects.

Those who thus wisely see the difference between the objects, and their knower find their freedom from bondage and become self-actualized persons.

This is another chapter devoted to describe the nature of the subject, the object, and the field of their interaction. It elaborates the indestructible nature of the eternal *self*. The *purusha* pervades all beings. All of us share the same *self*, which is the binding factor that bonds people. Divisions arise from the manifestations of *prakriti*, which is ever in the process of change and mutation. From a counselling perspective, the therapist should be on the look out to explore factors that build rapport and amity between the client and the people with whom he comes into contact.

14

The Three Gunas and Beyond

KRISHNA continues his counsel to Arjuna:

Once again, I will expound for your benefit the highest wisdom that sages displayed in order to reach the state of self-actualization.

Gaining such wisdom, they have attained divinity; they are eternal and beyond the process of manifestation and dissolution of the empirical world.

Prakriti is the womb in which the cosmic embryo is implanted, from which the birth of all beings starts.

The transcendental womb is the great Absolute, *Brahman*. I am the father who impregnates and implants the seed.

The eternal spirit is imprisoned in the body due to the three *gunas* – *sattva, rajas,* and *tamas* – the constituents of *prakriti.*

Sattva illumines and heals one of all ills. It is the *guna* that makes one happy and virtuous by bestowing right knowledge.

Rajas is passion; it is the main source of craving and attachment. It binds the spirit, imprisons it in the body, and engenders attachment to actions.

Tamas is born out of congenital ignorance, and is

the cause of all kinds of delusions. It is the source of manifest negligence, inactivity, sleep, and stupor.

Sattva causes attachment to pleasure. *Rajas* prompts action; and *tamas* shrouds knowledge and makes one prone to error.

When *sattva* dominates, passion and proneness to error are under check. When *rajas* prevails, goodness as well as indolence are overpowered. When *tamas* takes over, the opposite happens; happiness and activity take the back seat.

Sattva may be seen as dominant, when knowledge springs from all the senses in the body.

With the increase of *rajas*, there arise accelerated activity, unrest and craving.

Gloom, inertness, error and delusion descend on one when *tamas* dominates.

If *sattva* prevails at the time of one's death, the *self* moves closer to knowing the truth in the births to follow.

At the time of one's death, if passion (*rajas*) is dominant in the mind, he would be reborn with attachment to action; if *tamas* prevails, he would be born ignorant, prone to error.

Virtuous actions are a result of one's sattvic nature; pain follows rajasic conduct; and ignorance is a product of *tamas*.

Knowledge is the outcome of *sattva guna*; greed and craving are associated with *rajas*; and negligence and error accompany *tamas*.

Those who cultivate *sattva,* move closer to self-actualization; tamasic persons move farther away from it; and rajasic people stay in the middle.

When a person perceives that no person is truly the agent behind the manifestations in the world and realizes that divinity is beyond the appearances, he reaches a state of self-actualization.

Realization that the *gunas* are the result of the bodily functions and not of the *spirit* liberates the person from birth, death, old age, and pain, and makes him immortal.

Arjuna goes on to ask:

What are the characteristics of the person who transcends the three *gunas*? How does he live? How does he rise above the *gunas* to reach divinity?

Krishna answers:

The enlightened one does not despise illumination; he does not discard action, nor does he crave for them when they cease to exist.

He is unconcerned, undisturbed, and unaffected by the manifestations of nature, knowing that they are mere appearances.

He treats pain and pleasure alike. He does not differentiate between cold, stone or a piece of gold. He remains unperturbed amidst pleasant or unpleasant things. He endures pain and pleasure undaunted, because he finds refuge in his true *self.*

He who transcends the three *gunas* is unmoved by honour or dishonour that comes in his way; and he

> has no craving or attachment for achievements.
>
> He has unfailing devotion and commitment to divinity.
>
> The *Brahman*, absolute and unchanging, is lasting righteousness and endless bliss. He is grounded in the divinity that I revealed to you, Arjuna.

This chapter underscores the multifarious manifestations of *prakriti* with its inherent three *gunas*. It describes the characteristic conduct and behaviour of people when one of the three *gunas* asserts its domination. A self-actualized person knows that the *gunas* are attributes of *prakriti* and not of *purusha*. With undiminished devotion to the spirit, he becomes enlightened and learns how to overcome dichotomies and diversities. He cultivates knowledge without discarding action. The lesson one gets from this passage is that beliefs and conduct, thought and action should go hand in hand. Any confrontation between them is likely to have adverse effects on one's mental health.

15

The Spirit Supreme

Continuing his discourse, Krishna explains the nature of the transcendental spirit that resides in and binds people together.

> The truth-realizing sages refer to the mystic fig tree with its roots above and leaves below the ground. Indeed the leaves are the Vedas. The one who realizes this has the genuine knowledge of the Vedas.
>
> The branches grow below and above the ground because of the three *gunas*. The objects of senses are the shoots above. Below are the root-sprouting actions.
>
> The appearance of form, its foundation, beginning, and the end disappear, once they are cut-off by the sword of detachment.
>
> Therefore, one must find the way to the eternal from which there is no return, seeking refuge in the transcendental, from which emanates the cosmic process.
>
> Free from pride and ego-indulgence, avoiding the evil of attachment, controlling all desires, ever-devoted to the Divine, overcoming the perception of such dualities as pain and pleasure, and not deluded by appearances one reaches the state of self-actualization.

There is no need for the sun, the moon, or fire to illuminate the abode of the Divine. It is self-luminous. When one reaches there, there is no return for him.

A small fragment of the eternal *Self* pervades all the manifest beings in the world. Embodied it attracts the senses, including the mind which are part of *prakriti.*

Like the wind which takes the perfumes it touches, the embodied *self* (*purusha*) carries with it the mind and the senses when it takes another birth.

The person perceives the objects through the five senses and the mind.

Those deluded by the appearances perpetuated by the three *gunas* do not become aware that the *self* is indeed the real source. One needs the eye of wisdom to see the *self* within.

People with wisdom, who persevere, see the *self* situated at the core of their being. However, the not-so-wise fail to become aware of the self despite their persistent efforts.

The splendour of the blazing sun, the shining moon, and the burning fire radiate from the Divine.

The illuminating divine sun sustains all beings on the earth; the shine of the moon nourishes all plants and herbs.

The fire of hunger in living human bodies along with breathing in and out help digest all kinds and modes of food intake.

The Divine takes its abode in the hearts of living bodies. From this spring forth memory and knowledge, as well as forgetfulness. Vedas are an attempt to understand and describe me. Indeed I am the source of the Vedanta. I am also the knower of the Vedas.

The world has two aspects: perishable and imperishable. The perishable are the changing appearances. The imperishable is the self (*purusha*) inside.

In addition to this changing and perishable world, there is the immutable *Spirit* that sustains the world in its manifest forms.

That immutable, eternal *spirit* is truly the divine state.

He who knows the supreme spiritual nature behind the apparent manifestations, without any delusions and with complete devotion attains divinity.

I have thus revealed to you my cosmic nature. Gaining such knowledge, one becomes wise and performs his duties undaunted.

Krishna explains to Arjuna the transcendental aspects of being. Such knowledge enables one to perform without any hesitation, his actions wisely, and in consonance with ethical norms. The emphasis once again is on the Divine. The *purusha* is the Divine spirit embodied in the person. The ego is a manifestation of the mind, an evolute of *prakriti*. It renders the mind less reliable and moves it further from truth. In the context of counselling, the therapist should attempt to make the client become better aware of the ego that it misleads and creates wrong perceptions.

16

The Attributes of Divine, Daring, and Devilish States

KRISHNA says:

Courage, purity of mind, perpetual pursuit of knowledge, charity, self-control, sacrifice, understanding scriptures, engaging in ascetic practices, and uprightness,

nonviolence, truthfulness, free from anger and envy, renunciation, peacefulness, gentleness, modesty, dignity, and being steady and steadfast,

brilliance, persistence, and free from the ego and pride are the characteristics of the person who becomes aware of embodied divinity.

On the other hand, hypocrisy, unworthy pride and needless anger, harshness, and lack of knowledge are the characteristics of the devilish state.

Cultivation of divine states is conducive for gaining ultimate freedom whereas indulgence in devilish acts makes the person fettered further.

As mentioned, there are three types among people in the world – the divine, the devilish, and those in between. I have described at some length the divine attributes. I will now dwell upon the demonic characteristics.

A demonic person does not know how to act upright, nor does he know the way of renunciation. He is not clean at heart. His conduct is shady; he is not truthful.

He believes that this world is unreal and ungrounded, without any good reason. For him there is no God. The happenings of the world have no causal roots in one's desires. People in his view are born out of the union of man and woman out of lust.

Committing themselves to these views, with little understanding of the true nature of things, such feeble-minded persons stand out pointedly as the true enemies of the world wishing its destruction.

Indulging in insatiable desires, hypocritical and envious, full of undeserving pride and vanity, and deluded, they behave without regard to morality.

Possessed by enormous aspirations, which would end only with their death, they act with impunity to gratify their desires. They are certain that there is nothing beyond sensory pleasures to make them happy.

They are driven by hundredfold desires to accumulate wealth for enjoyment in the present and for the future, thinking that all the wealth belongs to them.

They believe that this wealth they accumulate is theirs, and that it will be with them and make them.

Today, I killed my enemy; I will destroy any others who come in my way. I am successful, happy and powerful;

I am rich; and there is no one who excels me. I will

do with my money whatever I choose to do. Thinking thus, these people are deluded and ignorant of the truth behind all these manifestations.

Imaging in myriad similar ways, deluded, falling prey to lust and sensory gratification, they go to damned hell.

They are ego-driven, persistent in their pursuit of sensory enjoyment, conceited by pride and arrogance. They worship with ostentation and without regard to the prescribed rituals. They are indeed hypocrites.

Those who seek self-indulgence, power and pride with lust and wrath are malicious. They disregard divinity dwelling in them and others.

I throw such cruel creatures into the wombs of demons in their cycle of births and deaths to come.

These damned beings continue to be deluded and do not become self-actualized persons.

Lust, anger, and desire destroy the *spirit* and lead the person to hell. Therefore, one should avoid them.

The man who overcomes them becomes spiritual and is on his way to become a self-actualized person.

On the other hand, he who abandons the spiritual path and becomes a slave to his desires finds neither happiness now, nor liberation later.

Therefore, one's conduct should be ethical. Following the moral dictates one should act and perform his duties.

Krishna describes the manifestations of the three *gunas*

in people's conduct. The persons with sattvic disposition tend to be truthful, nonviolent, steadfast, non-egoistic, morally upright, gentle, and peaceful. Rajasic people are proud of their positions, envious of others, tend to be impulsive, aggressive and ambitions, and seek mostly sensory gratification. People with tamasic tendencies have no faith in God or divinity. They are feeble minded, ignorant of truth, slothful, and destructive. For the counsellor, the three *gunas* provide the basis for charting the personality profile of the client. They serve the purpose of giving necessary clues and insights into the way the client may act and react.

17

Three Ways of Becoming a Self-Actualized Person

ARJUNA continues to raise questions. He asks Krishna:

> What about those people who are ignorant of prescribed rituals, but make their devoted offerings? Are they prompted by *sattva guna*, *rajas* or *tamas*?

Krishna answers:

> The beliefs of the embodied beings born out of their inherent nature are of three kinds – sattvic, rajasic, or tamasic. Now let me explain how this works.
>
> The beliefs of each person are in accordance with their inherent nature, whether sattvic, rajasic, or tamasic. Their inherent nature prompts them to behave as they do. Their faith makes them what they are.
>
> Sattvic persons worship the divine gods and the rajasic people pray to pseudo-gods or the devils. The tamasic persons take refuge in evil spirits and ghosts.
>
> The devilish people, full of lust and cravings, hypocritical and egoistical, perform terrible austerities, which are not prescribed by scriptures. They disregard the Divine within. They are unwise and foolish.
>
> Even the foods which we fondly consume are of three

kinds. So are the offerings we make, the gifts we give, and the austerities we observe.

Sattvic persons are attracted to foods conducive to good health, which nurture their bodies and strengthen their mind, and give them real pleasure and comfort.

The foods the people with rajasic temperament enjoy are exceedingly bitter, hot, salty, and sour. They cause pain, suffering, and bad health.

Tamasic people eat food ill-prepared, tasteless, stale, and decomposed with bad odour.

Sattvic persons provide food for others without consuming it themselves. They expect nothing in return.

People with rajasic temperament feed others expecting some reward for it.

Tamas-dominant people, who are uninspired by spiritual prescriptions, offer no food to any sincerely.

There are three kinds of discipline to condition one's body. First is the worship of gods, teachers, and wise men. Second is observing cleanliness; and the third is being upright and ethical in conduct.

Disciplining one's utterances involves speaking truthfully with no offence to others, saying words that are pleasant, pleasing and helpful to others, and reciting the Vedas regularly.

Mental discipline involves observing serenity, silence, and self-control, and entertaining clean thoughts.

Good (sattvic) people observe the above threefold discipline without expecting anything as reward.

Rajasic people are engaged in these practices with expectation of reward. They are hypocrites. Their practices are not stable and lasting.

The tamasic people do their practices foolishly and stubbornly either by torturing themselves or injuring others.

Sattvic persons make their gifts at the right place and time to deserving people, who cannot return any favour, considering it as one's duty to help.

People with rajasic disposition when they offer a gift, they expect something in return to their advantage.

The gifts of *tamas*-predominant people go to unworthy people at wrong place or time.

The Absolute *Brahman* is addressed in three ways – *om*, *tat*, and *sat*. This is ordained in the Vedas and chanted by priests.

Therefore, all the sacred rituals begin with the chanting of *om*.

Offerings to gods and various acts of giving to others commence with the utterance of the term *tat*.

Sat connotes existence and righteousness. It denotes noble conduct.

Further, *sat* refers to steadfastness in service and sincerity in doing penance and giving gifts.

No matter what the gift is or the penance performed or the rituals practised, if they are without faith in divinity, they are considered unreal; and not of any consequence now or later.

This chapter describes the characteristics of people with different dispositions arising out of the dominant *gunas*. It goes on to give information even about different kinds of food that appeal to people with diverse dispositions. A possible implication is that what one eats may contribute towards developing one's temperament. From a counsellor's perspective, what one prefers to eat may be symptomatic of the underlying tendency problems, even though the family tradition and values could also be very relevant.

18

Renunciation and Self-Actualization

ARJUNA asks Krishna:

Oh Krishna, kindly enlighten me on the real difference between *sannyasa* (renunciation) and *tyaga* (relinquishment).

Krishna responds:

Renunciation means giving up of action motivated by desire, whereas relinquishment is abandoning the fruits of action.

According to some, all action should be given up as evil. Some others argue that actions such as oblation, giving gifts, and practice of austerities may not be stopped.

Now, I explain to you, Arjuna, the true meaning behind relinquishment.

One may not stop giving gifts, performing austerities, or offering oblation, because they help purify the acts of wise men.

However, these actions should be undertaken without attachment or desire for their fruits.

Giving up one's duties is not renunciation. Such abandonment is born out of ignorance. It is of the nature of *tamas*.

If one gives up action due to bodily exhaustion or because it is troublesome, he is a person dominated by rajasic nature.

The sattvic person does his work without attachment to or desire for its fruits.

The sattvic person, intelligent and without any doubt, does not crave for or cling to agreeable work; he does not hate and despise non-beneficial actions.

Embodied, man cannot totally abstain from work. However, the one who gives up the fruits of action is truly the relinquisher.

The consequences of one's actions are threefold - agreeable, disagreeable, or a mix of the two.

Arjuna, recall the five factors mentioned by the Samkhya system as conducive to accomplishment of good deeds.

They are the field, the doer, different instruments of action, and multi-various efforts, along with supernatural providence.

These five factors are involved in all actions one performs with his body, speech, or mind.

This being the truth, the man with a deluded mind lacking proper understanding, and unmindful of the truth thinks that he is the sole agent involved in bringing about these things.

The one who transcends the impulses of the ego, who has the right understanding, his actions whether destructive or constructive, would not bind him.

Knowledge, the object of knowledge, and the agent of knowledge constitute the threefold composite of work.

Thought, action, and their agent are three aspects of the *gunas*. Let me elucidate further.

Sattva is the element behind all knowledge. It enables one to know the single, unchanging substance that supports all existence.

Knowledge generated by *rajas* makes one aware of the multiplicity of the world, that it is divisible and consists of various kinds of things.

Tamas leads one to get attached and committed to a single manifest form of nature without regard to the system as a whole in its entirety.

Like knowledge, action is of three kinds. Action performed as duty with love and no ill-will, and detached from the ensuing consequences, is prompted by the sattvic component in one's nature.

Strenuous and egoistic actions to gratify one's desires are a result of the dominance of *rajas*.

Blind and deluded actions without concern for the consequences, whether they would cause injury or incur loss, are performed by the tamasic people.

The sattvic person performs his work without any attachment or ego-involvement, and with commitment, enthusiasm, and unmoved by success or failure.

The rajasic person is greedy, violence-prone, unclean, and attracted to the fruits of his actions.

The person of tamasic nature is not balanced. He is vulgar, obstinate, deceitful, evil-minded, slothful, desperate, and procrastinating.

There are three kinds of knowing and steadfastness born out of the three *gunas*.

Sattvic persons realize the difference between action and inaction, what should be undertaken and what should be avoided, what is to be feared and not to be feared, and what binds and what does not bind.

Rajasic individuals fail to appropriately differentiate the right from the wrong, good from evil, what one ought to do, and that which to avoid.

Tamasic people, blinded by the darkness of ignorance, look at things in a perverted way, mistaking the right for the wrong, and vice versa.

When *sattva* dominates, one is able to focus his mind, make it steadfast, and control his breath and sensory functions.

With the dominance of *rajas*, a person does his work, seeking pleasure and wealth, and for enjoying its fruits.

Persons enveloped in *tamas* tend to be slothful and are prone to fear, grief, depression, and indulgence.

There are three kinds of happiness. The first one is cultivated by constant practice.

Such happiness, which accrues from continued practice to realize the self, though it appears in the beginning like poison, it finally tastes like nectar. It is the manifestation of sattvic element.

Happiness arising out of sensory contact with the objects of the world may appear first as nectar, but it ends up as poison.

Tamasic happiness of the deluded person has its roots in sleep and originates from error and negligence.

No one in this world or heaven or among gods is devoid of these *gunas*, which are all-pervasive.

The duties of people belonging to different castes are so designated as to take into consideration the dominance of one or another of the three constituents of *prakriti*.

Brahmins constitute that class of people who are serene and are able to restrain their mind, control their senses, and observe necessary austerities. They are serene, self-controlled, clean and guiltless, and have knowledge of and faith in the scriptures.

Courage, strength, determination, skill, uprightness, wisdom, and uncompromising faith in scriptural commandments are the characteristics of people belonging to kshatriya clan.

The duties of vaishya class include cultivation of land, rearing cattle, and trade.

By fully committing oneself to his duties, a person becomes self-actualized.

Through performance of one's duties with devotion and by worshipping the Absolute from whence all beings find their existence, and which pervades the entire universe, one breaks all shackles and finds his true freedom.

Observing one's own prescribed duties, even imperfectly, is better than scrupulously performing the duties of others.

So, Arjuna, one should not give up actions warranted by one's own disposition even if they are not done perfectly. It is because all activities are shrouded, just like fire is hidden by smoke.

The one whose mind is detached from the objects of sensory enjoyment, self-controlled, and desireless becomes self-actualized by renouncing all actions.

Now, let me move on to explain how a man with consummate wisdom realizes the state of self-actualization.

Endowed with wisdom, exercising self-control with determination, discarding sensory contact, being indifferent to attraction or aversion;

cultivating the habit of living alone, eating as little as required, controlling thought, action, and passion, always engaged in meditation;

giving up egoistic actions, power, and pride, desire, anger and possessiveness with equanimity, the truth seeker moves towards self-actualization.

The self-actualized person, with a steady mind is at peace. He has no desires or grievances. He acts with commitment without any discrimination.

He realizes truth; and has proper understanding of divinity and how to reach the divine state.

Performing his duties regularly without a break and

with full faith, he finds his way to the unchanging, transcendental realm.

Giving up all wanderings of the mind with full faith in divinity, he focuses his mind relentlessly and with steadfastness on the lasting and unchanging Supreme Being.

With a focused mind, he crosses all the hurdles on the way. Lacking such a focus on divinity one perishes.

Deluded, if you, Arjuna, think of not fighting, it would be in vain, because your true nature would compel you to fight.

You shall fight, even if that were contrary to what your deluded mind thinks, because it is in your nature to fight and not to flee.

The divine will pervades all beings; it makes them move like a wheel in the machine set in motion by *maya*.

Arjuna, seek your refuge in the Divine with devotion and complete resolve. You will have lasting peace and happiness.

I have revealed to you thus the sacred knowledge as I understand it. Now, you do what you consider as appropriate.

Again here is a summary of the thoughts shrouded in mystery for so long, which I have now revealed to you because I thought that it would do good to you.

Focus your mind with full faith and resolve, and you will surely realize the divine state. You are very close to it.

> Abandoning all activities, find your shelter in the Divine. You need to have no regret; you will be free from all evils.
>
> This secret I revealed to you may not be disclosed to anyone who is not austere in his life, who has no faith in divinity, and does not obey the dictates of the Divine and decries it; because they may abuse it.
>
> Those who transmit this transcendental wisdom with true devotion will doubtless find their way to divinity.
>
> No one is more near and dear to the Divine than the one who undertakes such actions without any attachment or desire.
>
> Those who understand this sacred dialogue between us are Divine worshippers with true knowledge.
>
> The man who studies this dialogue with unwavering faith or listens to these sermons becomes a self-actualized person.
>
> Have you, Arjuna, assimilated this message? Does it clear your mind of all confusion and perplexities caused by ignorance?

The quintessence of the concluding chapter of the *Bhagavadgita* is the assertion that unselfish action, without attachment or aversion, is the sure way for achieving a state of self-actualization. In fact, it is the central thesis of the *Gita*. Therefore, the message of the *Gita* has unending relevance to the person as well as to the society of which he is a part. It reflects in many ways the reflexivity of the individual and the society and reinforces the fact that one is the mirror of the other.

The all-embracing principle underlying the *Gita* is that renunciation in and not of action is what leads one on the path of self-actualization. It is to be expected that the mind, despite focused attention, gets distracted and disturbed occasionally. Therefore, in addition to knowledge, devotion and commitment are called for, and one needs to constantly keep them in mind and to continuously cultivate them. Such relentless devotion helps one to overcome the ever-present distractions.

Satisfied with Krishna's counsel Arjuna says:

> My mind is now clear without any confusion. My memory of truth is back with your blessings. I am steadfast, and shall act in accordance with your instructions.

Sanjaya to Dhritarashtra, the blind king:

> In this way, I had the privilege of becoming aware of this marvellous and thrilling dialogue between Arjuna and Krishna.
>
> Due to the blessings of Sage Vyasa, I learnt the secret of supreme *yoga* from none other than the divine Krishna.
>
> I rejoice repeatedly recalling this sacred dialogue between Arjuna and Krishna.
>
> My happiness is limitless as I reminisce this most marvellous dialogue.
>
> Wherever, the great master of *yoga* Krishna and the unrivaled warrior Arjuna are, there shall be glory, success, prosperity, steadfastness, and stability without any disorder.

The sacred song of the Hindus, the *Bhagavadgita*, thus concludes with an exhortation to learn from it and to spread its message around for the welfare one's being and for the good of the society.

Index